contents

Lofoten Island Sweater

•••

Cod fishing on the Lofoten Islands of northern Norway provided the inspiration
for this infant sweater that features a fishtail pattern on the bottom, fishnet
and waves on the body, and Codfish drying on racks on the yoke. It is knit
in the traditional Norwegian style—in the round with a steek for the sleeve,
which is sewn and cut later to make the armhole.

Design by Sue Flanders

Sizes
6 (9, 12, 18, 24) months

Finished Measurements
Chest: 18½ (19½, 20¼, 21¼, 22¼)"/27 (49.5,
51.5, 54, 56.5)cm
Length: 11¼ (11¾, 12¼, 12¼, 12¾)"/28.5 (30,
31, 31, 32.5)cm

Materials
 DK weight; 100% superwash
merino wool; 120 yds/131m per 1¾
oz/50g skein): 2 (2, 2, 3, 3) skeins light navy
(A), 2 (3, 3, 4, 4) skeins light blue (B), 1 skein
dark blue (C)

Size 4 (3.5mm) double-pointed and
16"/40cm circular needles or size needed
to obtain gauge

Stitch markers

Waste yarn or stitch holders

Tapestry needle

Sewing machine

Gauge
26 sts and 28 rnds = 4"/10cm in stranded
2-color St st.
*Adjust needle size as necessary to obtain
correct gauge.*

Special Technique

3-needle bind-off: With RS tog and needles parallel, using a 3rd needle, knit tog a st from the front needle with 1 from the back. *Knit tog a st from the front and back needles, and slip the first st over the 2nd to bind off. Rep from * across, then fasten off last st.

Pattern Notes

The body is worked in-the-round, from the bottom up.

5 extra steek stitches are added between the front and back for the armholes. Work the steek stitches as follows: K2A, k1CC, k2A, where CC is either B or C depending on the pattern round being worked. (On single-color round, work with whatever color is being used.) The steek stitches are sewn with a sewing machine and then cut to make the armhole openings.

The neck is shaped after the sweater is worked by machine stitching a curved line at center front, then cutting out the fabric inside the machine stitching.

Dotted lines on schematics show cut edges. All cut edges have facings covering them.

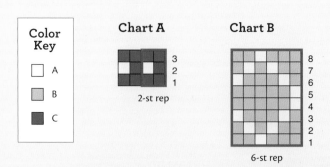

Chart C

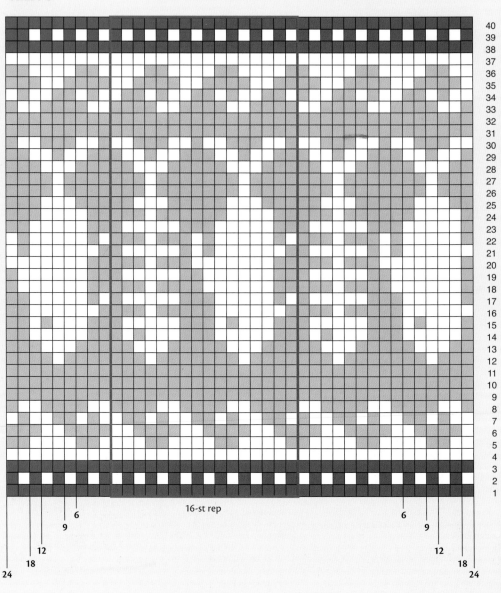

••• Instructions

Body

With smaller circular needle and C, CO 120 (126, 132, 138, 144) sts. Pm for beg of rnd and join, taking care not to twist sts.

Work Fishtail pat as follows:

Rnds 1–3: With C, *k2, yo, k2, k2tog; rep from * around.

Rnds 4–7: With B, *k2, yo, k2, k2tog; rep from * around.

Rnds 8–11: With A, *k2, yo, k2, k2tog; rep from * around.

Rnds 12–15: Rep Rnds 4-7.

Rnd 16: With C, knit around.

Work 3-rnd Chart A.

Work 8-rnd Chart B until piece measures 5½ (6, 6½, 6½, 7)"/14 (15.25, 16.5, 16.5, 17.75)cm, ending after Rnd 4 or 8.

Yoke

Rnd 1 (establish steeks): *With C, CO 5 sts for underarm steek; beg where indicated for your size, work 60 (63, 66, 69, 72) front sts following Chart C; rep from * for back.

Continue working Chart C and steek sts until 40-rnd chart is complete.

Thread all sts onto waste yarn.

Sleeves

With dpns and B, CO 36 sts; mark beg of rnd and join, taking care not to twist sts.

Work 16-rnd Fishtail pat as for Body, and on last rnd, inc 1 st at beg of rnd—37 sts.
Note: This extra st is the center underarm and is not included in the charted pattern. On any rnds that use A, knit with A. If rnd is worked without A, knit with whatever color is being used.

Next rnd: K1; work Chart A around rem 36 sts.

Next 2 rnds: Complete Chart A.

Next rnd: K1A; work Rnd 1 of Chart B around.

Next rnd (inc): K1A, M1, work Rnd 2 of Chart B to end, M1—39 sts.
Note: Work M1s using color that will maintain the pat, and work all inc'd sts on following rnd in expanded pat.

Continue working Chart B and M1 on each side of the center underarm st [every 2 rnds] 12 (11, 8, 2, 2) times, then [every 4 rnds] 2 (3, 6, 12, 12) times—67 sts.

Work even until sleeve measures approx 7 (7½, 8½, 10, 10½)"/18 (19, 21½, 25½, 26½)cm or ½"/1.25cm short of desired length.

Work 3-rnd Chart A.

Sleeve Facing

With C, work sleeve facing back and forth in reverse St st as follows:

Rows 1 and 3 (RS): Purl.

Rows 2 and 4: Knit.

BO loosely, with larger needle.

Finishing

Wet-block pieces.

Stabilize Steek Stitches

Set sewing machine to small sts. Place yoke under the machine foot and sew on column of sts adjacent to the center CC column of steek sts, beg at shoulder and ending at steek CO. Turn and sew back along column of sts on other side of CC column. It is important to sew into a column of sts and not in the "ladders" between the sts to make a much stronger steek. Sew at least 3 rows on each side of the CC sts.

Cut open armhole along CC line.

Rep for other armhole.

Right Shoulder Seam

Turn body inside out and transfer yoke sts to 2 circular needles. Join 20 (21, 22, 23, 24) right shoulder sts using 3-needle BO.

Transfer next 20 (21, 22, 23, 24) front and back sts to separate holders for neck; transfer rem 20 (21, 22, 23, 24) sts to separate holders for left shoulder.

Front Neckline

Mark a position 1½ (1¾, 2, 2¼, 2½)"/4 (4.5, 5, 5.5, 6.5) cm down from center front neck. Baste a curved line from this low point to the points where the shoulder sts meet the neck sts for front neck opening. Use sewing machine to sew along the marked front neck, sewing at least 3 rows with the machine.

Cut out neckline semicircle inside the machine stitching.

Buttonhole Band

Transfer back shoulder sts to needle.

Row 1 (RS): Join C; purl across.

Row 2: Work in k1, p1 rib across.

Schematics

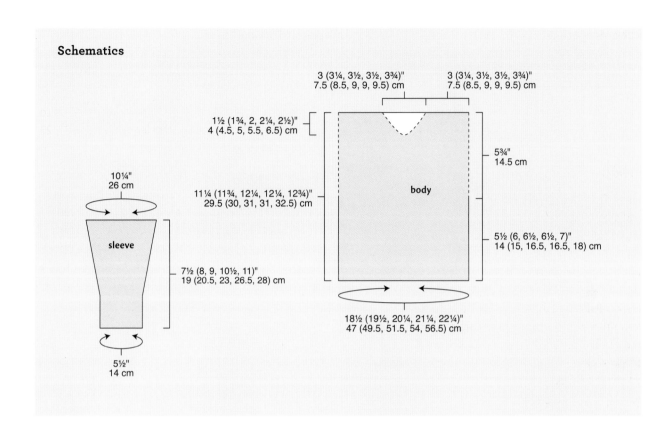

3 (3¼, 3½, 3½, 3¾)"
7.5 (8.5, 9, 9, 9.5) cm

3 (3¼, 3½, 3½, 3¾)"
7.5 (8.5, 9, 9, 9.5) cm

1½ (1¾, 2, 2¼, 2½)"
4 (4.5, 5, 5.5, 6.5) cm

5¾"
14.5 cm

10¼"
26 cm

11¼ (11¾, 12¼, 12¼, 12¾)"
29.5 (30, 31, 31, 32.5) cm

body

sleeve

5½ (6, 6½, 6½, 7)"
14 (15, 16.5, 16.5, 18) cm

7½ (8, 9, 10½, 11)"
19 (20.5, 23, 26.5, 28) cm

18½ (19½, 20¼, 21¼, 22¼)"
47 (49.5, 51.5, 54, 56.5) cm

5½"
14 cm

Buttonhole row: Maintain rib and work 3 [yo, k2tog] buttonholes evenly spaced along band.

Row 3: Work in established rib.

BO in rib.

Button Band Facing

Transfer front shoulder sts to needle.

Turning row 1 (RS): Join C; purl across.

Work 3 rows in St st.

Overlap button band with buttonhole band and tack in place at shoulder.

Join Sleeves

Sew sleeve into place along the line between steek sts and charted pat.

Sew facing to WS to cover the sewn steek edges.

Neck Edging

With RS facing and using C, pick up and knit approx 34 (35, 38, 40, 42) sts along front neck edge, knit across rem 20 (21, 22, 23, 24) back neck sts.

Row 1 (WS): Knit.

Rows 2–4: Work Chart A, back and forth.

Row 5 (turning row, WS): Knit.

Rows 7–8: Knit 1 row, purl 1 row, knit 1 row.

BO very loosely.

Sew facing to inside of neckline, folding along turning row.

Weave in all ends.

Block again.

Fair Isle Sweater

...

This little Fair Isle design has just enough patterning to make the knitting interesting and not too time-consuming. It's perfect as your first stranded knitting project.

Design by Melissa Leapman

Sizes
6 (12, 18) months

Finished Measurements
Chest circumference: 21 (24, 27)"/53.5 (61, 68.5)cm
Length: 11 (12, 13)"/28 (30.5, 33)cm

Materials

Sport weight; 100% superwash merino wool; 136 yds/124m per 1¾ oz/ 50g skein): 3 skeins periwinkle (A), 1 skein each apple green (B), purple (C), dark purple (D), and yellow (E)

Size 3 (3.25mm) needles

Size 5 (3.75mm) needles or size needed to obtain gauge

Stitch holders

Stitch markers

4 [½"/1.25cm] buttons

Gauge
24 sts and 32 rows = 4"/10cm in 2-color St st with larger needles.

Adjust needle size as necessary to obtain correct gauge.

Pattern Stitches

1×1 Rib (odd number of sts)

Row 1 (RS): K1, *p1, k1; rep from * to end.

Row 2: P1, *k1, p1; rep from * to end.

Rep Rows 1 and 2 for pat.

Fair Isle Chart

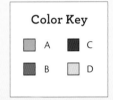

Color Key

▨	A	■	C
▨	B	□	D

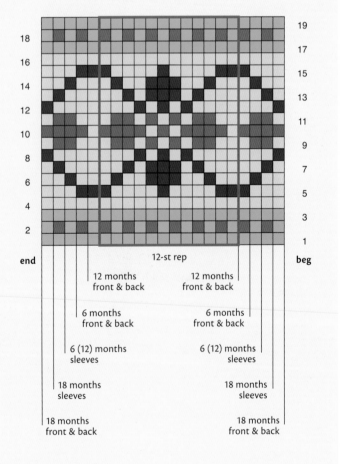

••• Instructions

Back

With smaller needles and A, CO 63 (73, 81) sts.

Work in 1×1 Rib for 1"/2.5cm, ending with a WS row.

Change to larger needles; beg and end where indicated for your size, work 19-row Fair Isle pat following chart. Cut all yarns.

With A, work even in St st until piece measures approx 11 (12, 13)"/28 (30.5, 33)cm, ending with a RS row.

Next row (WS): P20 (25, 26) sts and slip them onto a holder for button band; BO rem sts.

Front

Work same as for back until piece measures approximately 9½ (10½, 11½)"/24 (26.5, 29)cm, ending with a WS row.

Shape Neck

Next row (RS): K22 (27, 29); join 2nd ball of yarn and BO center 19 (19, 23) sts, knit to end of row.

Working both sides at once with separate balls of yarn, dec 1 st each neck edge every row 2 (2, 3) times—20 (25, 26) sts rem each side.

Work even, if necessary, until piece measures 10½ (11¼, 12¼)"/26.5 (28.5, 31)cm, ending with a WS row.

Next row (RS): Slip first 20 (25, 26) sts to holder for buttonhole band; knit to end of row.

Work even on rem side until it measures same as back.

BO.

Sleeves

With smaller needles and A, CO 41 (41, 43) sts.

Work in 1x1 Rib for 1"/2.5cm, ending with a WS row.

Change to larger needles; work 19-row Fair Isle pat, then continue with A only.

At the same time, inc 1 st each side [every 4 rows] 6 (8, 6) times, then [every 6 rows] 2 (2, 4) times, working new sts into pat as they accumulate—57 (61, 63) sts.

Work even until piece measures approx 6½ (7½, 8½)"/16.5 (19, 21.5)cm.

BO.

Finishing

Block pieces to finished measurements.

Sew right shoulder seam.

Neckband

With RS facing, using smaller needles and A, pick up and knit 56 (56, 60) sts along neckline.

Row 1 (WS): *K1, p1; rep from * across.

Work 8 rows in established rib.

BO in rib.

Button band

With RS of back facing, using smaller needles and A, pick up and knit 6 sts along side of neckband, then k20 (25, 26) buttonband sts from holder—26 (31, 32) sts.

Work 6 rows in k1, p1 rib.

BO in rib

Place markers for 4 evenly-spaced buttons on band, with the first and last ¼"/6mm from side edges.

Buttonhole Band

Transfer 20 (25, 26) buttonhole band sts to smaller needle.

With RS facing, smaller needles, and A, work 1×1 Rib across sts, then pick up and knit 6 sts along neckband—26 (31, 32) sts.

Work 1 row in established rib.

Buttonhole row (RS): Cont in rib and make buttonholes opposite each marker on buttonband by working (k2tog, yo).

Work 6 rows even.

BO in rib.

With buttonhole band overlapping button band, sew top of armhole closed.

Place markers 4¾ (5, 5¼)"/12 (12.5, 13.5)cm down from shoulders.

Sew on sleeves between markers.

Sew sleeve and side seams.

Sew on buttons.

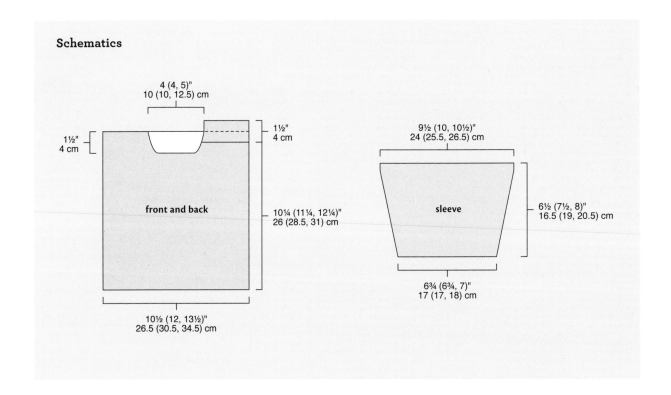

Schematics

4 (4, 5)"
10 (10, 12.5) cm

1½"
4 cm

1½"
4 cm

front and back

10¼ (11¼, 12¼)"
26 (28.5, 31) cm

10½ (12, 13½)"
26.5 (30.5, 34.5) cm

9½ (10, 10½)"
24 (25.5, 26.5) cm

sleeve

6½ (7½, 8)"
16.5 (19, 20.5) cm

6¾ (6¾, 7)"
17 (17, 18) cm

Aran Sweater

•••

This pullover has all the elements of a traditional Aran design in a pint-size piece.
Shaping is minimal so you can relax and enjoy knitting the textures.

Design by Melissa Leapman

Sizes
6 (12, 18) months

Finished Measurements
Chest: 20½ (24, 26½)"/52 (61, 67.5)cm
Length: 11 (12, 13)"/28 (30.5, 33)cm

Materials
 Worsted weight; 100% easy-care wool; 98 yds/90m per 1.75 oz/50g ball): 4 (5, 5) balls almond

Size 6 (4mm) needles

Size 8 (5mm) needles or size needed to obtain gauge

Cable needle

Stitch holders

4 [½"/1.25cm] buttons

Gauge
18 sts and 24 rows = 4"/10cm in Double Seed St with larger needles.
Adjust needle size as necessary to obtain correct gauge.

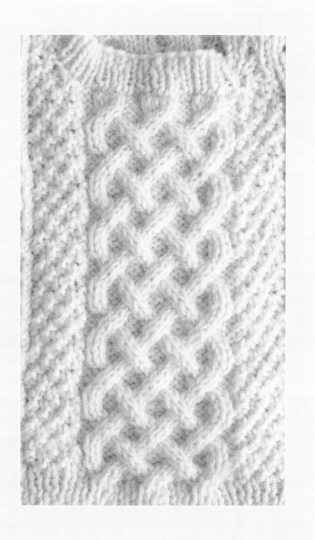

Special Abbreviations

2 over 2 Left Cross (2/2 LC): Slip 2 sts to cn and hold in front, k2, k2 from cn.

2 over 2 Right Cross (2/2 RC): Slip 2 sts to cn and hold in back, k2, k2 from cn.

2 over 2 Left Purl Cross (2/2 LPC): Slip 2 sts to cn and hold in front, p2, k2 from cn.

2 over 2 Right Purl Cross (2/2 RPC): Slip 2 sts to cn and hold in back, k2, p2 from cn.

Pattern Stitches

1x1 Rib (even number of sts)

Row 1 (RS): *K1, p1; rep from * to end.

Rep Row 1 for pat.

Seed Stitch (odd number of sts)

Row 1 (RS): K1, *p1, k1; rep from * to end.

Rows 2 and 3: P1, *k1, p1; rep from * to end.

Row 4: Rep Row 1.

Rep Rows 1–4 for pat.

Cable Panel A (12-st panel)

Row 1 (RS): P1, k1-tbl, p1, 2/2 RC, k2, p1, k1-tbl, p1.

Row 2: K1, p1-tbl, k1, p6, k1, p1-tbl, k1.

Row 3: P1, k1-tbl, p1, k2, 2/2 LC, p1, k1-tbl, p1.

Row 4: Rep Row 2.

Rep Rows 1–4 for pat.

Cable Panel B (26-st panel)

Row 1 (RS): P3, [2/2 RC, p4] twice, 2/2 RC, p3.

Row 2: K3, p4, [k4, p4] twice, k3.

Row 3: P1, [2/2 RPC, 2/2 LPC] 3 times, p1.

Row 4: K1, p2, [k4, p4] twice, k4, p2, k1.

Row 5: P1, k2, p4, [2/2 LC, p4] twice, k2, p1.

Row 6: Rep Row 4.

Row 7: P1, [2/2 LPC, 2/2 RPC] 3 times, p1.

Row 8: Rep Row 2.

Rep Rows 1–8 for pat.

Stitch Key

☐	k on RS, p on WS
⊟	p on RS, k on WS
⚇	k1-tbl on RS, p1-tbl on WS
⧅	2/2 RC
⧄	2/2 LC
◩	2/2 RPC
◪	2/2 LPC

Cable Panel A

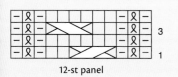

12-st panel

Cable Panel B

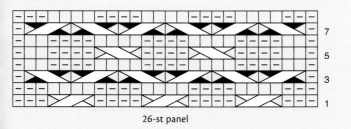

26-st panel

••• Instructions

Back

With smaller needles, CO 70 (78, 86) sts.

Work in 1×1 Rib for 1"/2.5cm, ending with a WS row.

Set-up row (RS): Change to larger needles; working Row 1 of each pattern, work Double Seed St across first 5 (9, 13) sts, pm, work Cable Panel A across next 12 sts, pm, work Double Seed St across next 5 sts, pm, work Cable Panel B across next 26 sts, pm, work Double Seed St across next 5 sts, pm, work Cable Panel A across next 12 sts, pm, work Double Seed St across last 5 (9, 13) sts.

Work even in established pats until piece measures approx 11 (12, 13)"/28 (30.5, 33)cm, ending with a RS row.

Next row (WS): Work across 20 (24, 26) sts and slip them onto holder for button band; BO rem sts.

Front

Work same as back until piece measures approximately 9½ (10½, 11½)"/24 (26.5, 29)cm, ending with a WS row.

Shape Neck

Next row (RS): Work across first 22 (26, 30) sts; join 2nd ball of yarn and BO center 26 sts, work to end of row.

Next 2 rows: Working both sides at once with separate balls of yarn, dec 1 st at each neck edge—20 (24, 28) sts rem each side.

Work even, if necessary, until piece measures 10¼ (11¼, 12¼)"/26 (28.5, 31)cm, ending with a WS row.

Next row (RS): Slip first 20 (24, 28) sts to holder for buttonhole band; work across rem sts.

Work even on this side until it measures same as back.

BO.

Sleeves

With smaller needles, CO 30 (30, 32) sts.

Work in 1×1 Rib for 1"/2.5cm, ending with a WS row, and on last row, inc 1 st at end of row—31 (31, 33) sts.

Change to larger needles and Double Seed St.

Inc 1 st each side [every 4 rows] 5 (8, 6) times, then [every 6 rows] 1 (0, 2) times, working new sts into pat as they accumulate—43 (47, 49) sts.

Work even until piece measures 6½ (7½, 8)"/16.5 (19, 20.5)cm.

BO.

Schematics

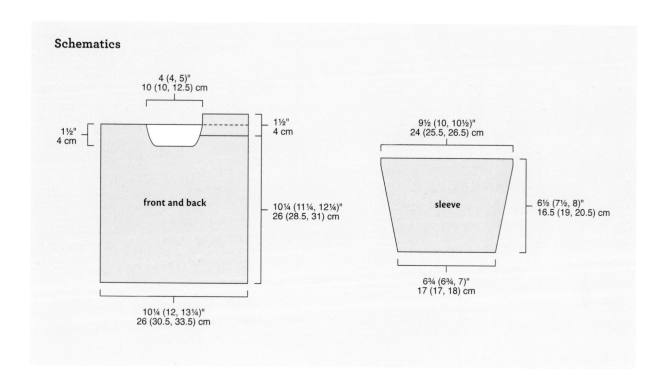

4 (4, 5)"
10 (10, 12.5) cm

1½"
4 cm

1½"
4 cm

front and back

10¼ (11¼, 12¼)"
26 (28.5, 31) cm

10¼ (12, 13¼)"
26 (30.5, 33.5) cm

9½ (10, 10½)"
24 (25.5, 26.5) cm

sleeve

6½ (7½, 8)"
16.5 (19, 20.5) cm

6¾ (6¾, 7)"
17 (17, 18) cm

Finishing

Block pieces to finished measurements.

Sew right shoulder seam.

Neckband

With RS facing and smaller needles, pick up and knit 56 (56, 60) sts along neckline.

Work in 1×1 Rib for 1"/2.5cm.

BO in rib.

Button band

With RS of back facing and smaller needles, pick up and knit 4 sts along side of neckband, work in 1×1 Rib across 20 (24, 28) button band sts from holder—24 (28, 32) sts.

Work 4 rows in 1×1 Rib.

BO in rib.

Place markers for 4 evenly-spaced buttons on band, with the first and last placed ¼"/6mm from side edges.

Buttonhole Band

Transfer 20 (24, 28) sts from buttonhole band sts to smaller needle.

With RS facing and smaller needles, work 1×1 Rib across sts, then pick up and knit 4 along side of neckband—24 (28, 32) sts.

Work 1 WS row in 1×1 Rib.

Buttonhole row (RS): Cont in rib and make buttonholes opposite each marker on button band by working (k2tog, yo).

Work 2 rows even.

BO in rib.

With buttonhole band overlapping button band, sew top of armhole closed.

Place markers 4¾ (5, 5¼)"/12 (12.5, 13.5)cm down from shoulders.

Sew on sleeves between markers.

Sew sleeve and side seams.

Sew on buttons.

Baby Kimono Sweater

•••

Worked in a gorgeous lucky red color, this cute jacket will keep your little one warm while still being stylish. It's suitable for intermediate-level knitters.

Design by Melissa Leapman

Sizes
6 (12, 24) months

Finished Measurements
Chest (closed): 20 (22, 24)"/51 (56, 61)cm
Length: 10 (10½, 11)"/25.5 (26.5, 28)cm

Materials

 Sport weight; 100% superwash merino wool; 136 yds/124m per 1¾ oz/50g skein): 4 (4, 5) skeins red

Size 3 (3.25mm) straight and double-pointed needles

Size 5 (3.75mm) needles or size needed to obtain gauge

Stitch markers

2 [1⅜"/3.5cm] buttons

3 snaps, ½"/1.25cm

Gauge
24 sts and 40 rows = 4"/10cm in Textured pat with larger needles.
Adjust needle size as necessary to obtain correct gauge.

Textured Pattern

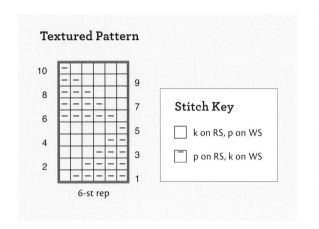

Stitch Key

- ☐ k on RS, p on WS
- ⊟ p on RS, k on WS

6-st rep

Pattern Stitch

Textured Pattern (*multiple of 6 sts*)

Row 1 (RS): *P5, k1; rep from * to end.
Row 2: *P2, k4; rep from * to end.
Row 3: *P3, k3; rep from * to end.
Row 4: *P4, k2; rep from * to end.
Row 5: *P1, k5; rep from * to end.
Row 6: *K5, p1; rep from * to end.
Row 7: *K2, p4; rep from * to end.
Row 8: *K3, p3; rep from * to end.
Row 9: *K4, p2; rep from * to end.
Row 10: *K1, p5; rep from * to end.
Rep Rows 1–10 for pat.

••• Instructions

Back

With smaller needles, CO 54 (60, 65) sts.

Knit 4 rows and inc 6 (6, 7) sts evenly across last row—60 (66, 72) sts.

Change to larger needles and Textured pat; work even until piece measures 10 (10½, 11)"/25.5 (26.5, 28)cm, ending with a WS row.

BO.

Right Front

With smaller needles, CO 49 (54, 60) sts.

Knit 4 rows and inc 5 (6, 6) sts evenly across last row—54 (60, 66) sts.

Change to larger needles and Textured pat; work even until piece measures 3 (3½, 3½)"/7.5 (9, 9)cm, ending with a WS row.

Shape Neck

Dec row (RS): K1, ssk, work to end of row—53 (59, 65) sts.

Dec row (WS): Work to last 3 sts, ssp, p1—52 (58, 64) sts.

Continue in established pat and rep last 2 rows 7 (9, 11) times, then dec on RS rows only 22 (20, 20) times—16 (20, 22) sts rem.

Work even until piece measures 10 (10½, 11)"/25.5 (26.5, 28)cm.

BO.

Left Front

Work as for right front to neck shaping

Shape Neck

Dec row (RS): Work to last 3 sts, k2tog, k1—53 (59, 65) sts.

Dec row (RS): P1, p2tog, work to end—52 (58, 64) sts.

Continue in established pat and rep last 2 rows 7 (9, 11) times, then dec on RS rows only 22 (20, 20) times—16 (20, 22) sts rem.

Work even until piece measures 10 (10½, 11)"/25.5 (26.5, 28)cm.

BO.

Sleeves

With smaller needles, CO 32 (32, 38) sts.

Knit 4 rows, and on last row, inc 4 sts evenly across—36 (36, 42) sts.

Change to larger needles and Textured pat.

Inc row (RS): K1, M1, work to last st, M1, k1—38 (38, 44) sts.

Rep Inc row [every RS row] 0 (3, 0) mores times, then [every 4 rows] 8 (8, 5) times, then [every 6 rows] 0 (0, 3) times, working new sts into pattern as they accumulate—54 (60, 60) sts.

Work even until sleeve measures 4¾ (5, 5¼)"/12 (12.5, 13.5) cm, ending with a WS row.

BO.

Finishing

Block all pieces to finished measurements.

Sew shoulder seams.

Place markers 4½ (5, 5)"/11.5, 12.5, 12.5)cm down from shoulders.

Sew on sleeves between markers.

Sew side and sleeve seams.

Lower Body Edging

Front and Neckline Edging

Pick-up row: With RS facing and using smaller needles, beginning at lower right front edge; pick up and knit 18 (21, 21) sts along flat section of right front, pm, 60 (60, 63) sts along right front neck opening, 26 (26, 28) sts along back of neck, 60 (60,

63) sts along left front neck opening, pm, 18 (21, 21) sts along flat section of left front—184 (188, 196) sts.

Row 1 (WS): Knit to marker, slip marker, M1, knit to next marker, M1, slip marker, knit to end—2 sts inc'd.

Row 2: Knit.

Bind-off row: Binding off across row, knit (and BO) to first marker, M1, knit (and BO) to next marker, M1, knit (and BO) to end.

Sew 3 snaps into place between WS of left front and RS of right front.

Sew 2 buttons to RS of left front edge above snaps (see photo for placement).

Schematics

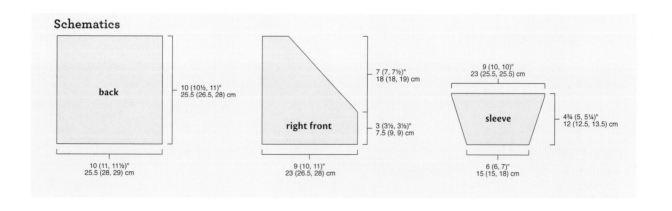

back
10 (10½, 11)"
25.5 (26.5, 28) cm
10 (11, 11½)"
25.5 (28, 29) cm

right front
7 (7, 7½)"
18 (18, 19) cm
3 (3½, 3½)"
7.5 (9, 9) cm
9 (10, 11)"
23 (26.5, 28) cm

sleeve
9 (10, 10)"
23 (25.5, 25.5) cm
4¾ (5, 5¼)"
12 (12.5, 13.5) cm
6 (6, 7)"
15 (15, 18) cm

Blueberry Forest Sweater

• • •

This toddler sweater was inspired by the landscape of the canoe country in the far northern part of Minnesota, where the mother and daughter designers go camping with their family. It's a place of paddling on lakes and camping on islands, cooking over fires and singing songs around them, hiking sunny hills and filling hats and water bottles with the small, delicious wild blueberries that grow among the wild roses and over the lichen-covered rocks. The trip that inspired this sweater took place just a year after a major forest fire had swept through the lake region. Already the shores were green, as the forest continued its slow growth, and the blueberries were particularly wonderful. The memories of that landscape provided the colors for this special design.

Design by Myra Arnold and Libby Johnson

Sizes

12 (24) months

Finished Measurements

Chest: 18 (20¾)"/46 (53)cm
Length: 11¾ (13¾)"/30 (35)cm

Materials
Size 12 months:

 Fingering weight; 100% wool; 180 yds/165m per 1¾ oz/50g skein): 2 skeins green (A), 1 skein each navy (B), medium blue (C), light blue (D), very light blue (E), avocado (F), brown (G); about 5 yds/5m yellow (H), and 2 yds/2m red (I)

Size 2 (2.75mm) 16"/40cm circular needle

Size 4 (3.5mm) 16"/40cm circular and double-pointed needles (set of 4) or size needed to obtain gauge

Size 24 months:

 Sport weight yarn; 100% wool; 164 yds/150m per 1¾ oz/50g skein): 2 skeins green (A), 1 skein each navy (B), medium blue (C), light blue (D), very light blue (E), avocado (F), brown (G); about 5 yds/5m yellow (H), and 2 yds/2m red (I)

Size 4 (3.5mm) 16"/40cm circular needle

Size 6 (4mm) 16"/40cm circular and double-pointed needles (set of 4) or size needed to obtain gauge

Both sizes:

Stitch markers

Tapestry needle

Sewing machine

6 [½"/1.25cm] buttons

Gauge

Size 12 months: 30 sts and 31 rnds = 4"/10cm in stranded 2-color St st using larger needle

Size 24 months: 26 sts and 27 rnds = 4"/10 cm in stranded 2-color St st using larger needle.
Adjust needle size as necessary to obtain correct gauge.

Pattern Notes

The pattern text is the same for both sizes, except for sleeve length. The 12-month size uses fingering weight yarn; the 24-month size uses sport weight yarn.

The sweater is worked in the round from the bottom up. Sleeve and bottom edges are hemmed.

There are 6 stitch steeks between the fronts and at the armholes, each of which will be cut open later. Work the steek stitches as follows: If two colors are used in a patterning round, alternate the colors in the steek. Keep the edge stitches at the beginning and end of steek in the same color as long as you are carrying that color. Change colors for next pattern round in the middle of the front steek. There is no need to weave in ends, just leave a 4"/10cm or so end hanging. If you are going to use that same color again in a few rows, you can let it hang at the steek and pick it up again when needed. All these ends will be secured when you sew the steek with a zigzag stitch on the sewing machine. Steek stitches are not included in the stitch counts.

The charted patterns don't necessarily use complete repeats. This makes no difference in the appearance of the sweater.

••• Instructions

Body

With smaller needles and C, CO 135 sts.

Work 6 rows back and forth in St st.

Turning ridge (RS): Purl.

Begin working in the round and set up front steek as follows: Pm, cast on 6 steek sts, pm, knit to end of rnd.

Knit 5 rnds.

Change to larger needle.

Work Rnds 1–41 of Chart A.

Divide for Armholes

Next rnd: Working Rnd 42 of Chart A, k32 for right front, BO 3 for underarm, k65 for back, BO 3 for underarm, k32 for left front, ending at front steek.

Next rnd (add armhole steeks): Working Rnd 43 of Chart A, knit across right front, pm, CO 6 sts for right armhole steek, pm; knit across back, pm, CO 6 sts for left armhole steek, pm; knit across left front.

Complete Chart A, working the 3 steeks between the markers.

Next rnd: Work Chart B across right front, work Chart C across back, work Chart D across left front.

Continue until 26-rnd charts are complete.

Change to Chart E and work 2 rnds, ending before the front steek.

Chart A

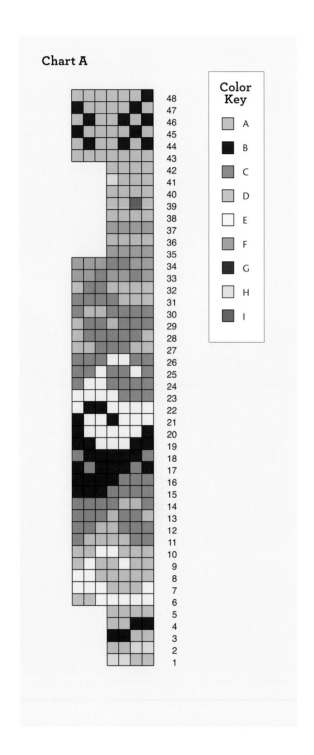

Color Key

- ☐ A
- ■ B
- ☐ C
- ☐ D
- ☐ E
- ☐ F
- ■ G
- ☐ H
- ■ I

Neck Shaping

Next rnd: Continuing Chart E, BO 6 steek sts; BO 4 right front sts, work in established pat to end, turn.

Begin working back and forth in rows, completing Chart E, and shape neck as follows:

BO 4 sts at beg of next row, then BO 3 sts at beg of next 3 rows.

Next row (WS): BO 3 sts, work across rem left front sts, work across steek, work 26 back sts, BO 13 sts for back neck, work to end of row—22 front sts and 26 back sts rem each side.

Transfer left front and left back shoulder sts to holder; continue working on right front and back sts only.

Right Front/Back Neck Shaping

Row 1 (RS): Ssk, work to end of row—21 front sts.

Row 2: BO 3, work to end of row—23 back sts.

Row 3: Work even.

Row 4: BO 2 sts, work to end—21 back sts.

Row 5: Work to marker, BO 6 steek sts, work to end.

With WS facing, join front and back shoulders using 3-needle BO.

Left Front/Back Neck Shaping

Transfer Left Front and Back sts to needle; with RS facing, rejoin yarn at back neck edge.

Row 1 (RS): BO3, work to end of row—23 back sts.

Row 2: P2tog, work to end of row—21 front sts.

Row 3: BO 2 sts, work to end—21 back sts.

Row 4: Work even.

Row 5: Work to marker, BO 6 steek sts, work to end.

With WS facing, join front and back shoulders using 3-needle BO.

Chart B (Right Front)

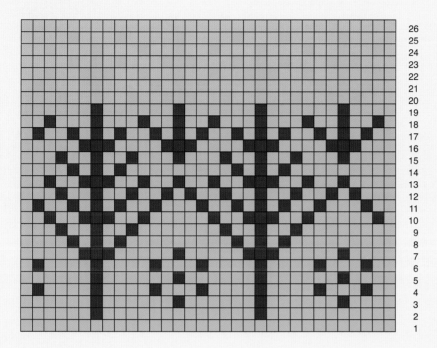

Color Key

  A

  D

■ G

Chart C (Back)

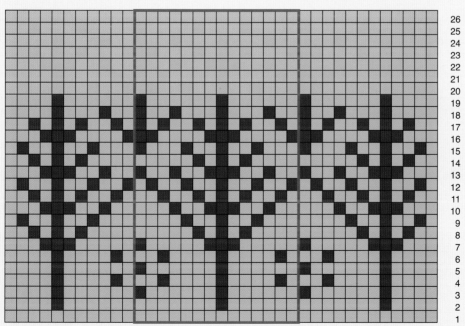

14-st rep

Chart D (Left Front)

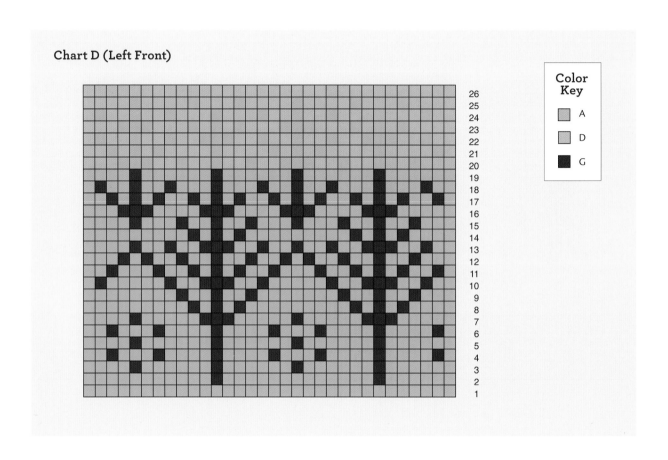

Color Key

- A
- D
- G

Neck Band

With RS facing and using smaller circular needle and E, pick up and knit 20 sts along right front neck, 38 sts along back neck, and 20 sts along left front neck—78 sts.

Row 1 (WS): P2, *k2, p2; rep from * to end.

Row 2: K2, *p2, k2; rep from * to end.

Rep Rows 1 and 2 twice more.

BO loosely in rib.

Cut Steeks

With smooth, brightly colored waste yarn, baste a line down the center of the front steek between sts 3 and 4. Using a sewing machine and zigzag st, carefully sew sts 2 and 3 tog; turn and sew sts 3 and 4 tog. With a sharp scissors, carefully cut along the basting line, making sure that you don't cut through the zigzag sts. Do the same for the armhole steeks.

Sleeves

With RS facing and using smaller dpns and E, beg at center underarm, pick up and knit 66 sts evenly around armhole, pm for beg of rnd and join. Change to larger needles.

Rnds 1–13: Work 13-rnd Chart E, beg at Rnd 13 and working to Rnd 1 to match shoulders.

Rnd 14: K1A, *k1E, k1A; rep from * around. Cut E.

Dec rnd: With A, k1, ssk, knit to last 3 sts, k2tog, k1—64 sts.

Chart E

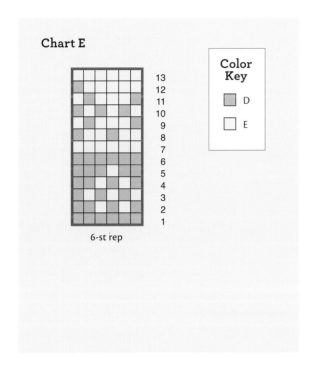

6-st rep

Color Key
- D
- E

Rep Dec rnd [every 4 rnds] 5 times, then [every other rnd] 5 times—42 sts.

Work even until sleeve measures 7 (7¾)"/18 (20)cm.

Cuff

Work 13-rnd Chart F.

Next rnd (turning ridge): With F, purl 1 rnd. Cut F.

Change to smaller needles and A.

Knit 14 rnds for sleeve hem.

BO very loosely. Cut yarn, leaving a very long tail.

Turn sleeve inside out and fold up hem along turning ridge.

Use tail to sew BO edge to WS of sleeve.

Buttonhole Band

Turn bottom hem up to WS along turning ridge; sew CO edge to WS.

With RS facing, using smaller needle and E, pick up and knit 68 sts along right front edge for girl (along left front edge for boy) in the first column of sts outside the steek. Pick-up rate is approx 7 sts for every 9 rows.

Row 1 (WS): P2, *k2, p2; rep from * to end.

Row 2 (RS): K2, *p2, k2; rep from * to end.

Row 3 (buttonhole row): P2, *yo, k2tog, p2, [k2, p2] twice; rep from * to last 6 sts, yo, k2tog, p2, k2.

Rows 4–5: Work in established rib.

BO loosely in rib.

Button Band

Work as for buttonhole band, picking up along opposite front and eliminating buttonholes.

Finishing

Fold cut ends of center steeks in toward inside of sweater body; sew down to body using crisscrossing sts.

Fold armhole steeks in toward body; sew down to body using criss-crossing sts.

Wash and block sweater to finished measurements. Tip: After wet sweater is positioned, whap it all over with a yardstick. This sounds strange, but it does the trick to gently flatten and smooth the knit fabric.

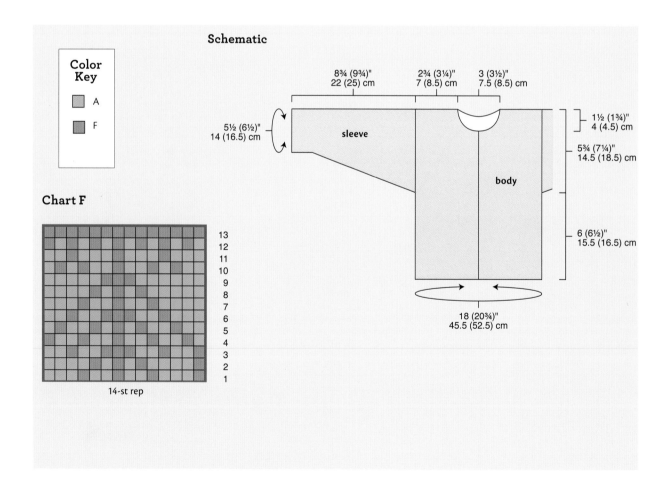

Knitting Abbreviations

beg	begin(s), beginning
BO	bind off
CC	contrast color
cm	centimeter(s)
CO	cast on
cont	continue, continuing
dec(s)	decrease, decreasing, decreases
dpn	double-pointed needle(s)
est	establish, established
foll	follow(s), following
inc(s)	increase(s), increasing
k	knit
k1f&b	knit into front then back of same st (increase)
k1f,b,&f	knit into front, back, then front again of same st (increase 2 sts)
k1-tbl	knit 1 st through back loop
k2tog	knit 2 sts together (decrease)
k2tog-tbl	knit 2 sts together through back loops
kwise	knitwise (as if to knit)
LH	left-hand
m(s)	marker(s)
MC	main color
mm	millimeter(s)
M1	make 1 (increase)
M1k	make 1 knitwise
M1p	make 1 purlwise
pat(s)	pattern(s)
p	purl
p1f&b	purl into front then back of same st (increase)
p1-tbl	purl 1 st through back loop
p2tog	purl 2 sts together (decrease)
pm	place marker
psso	pass slip st(s) over
pwise	purlwise (as if to purl)
rem	remain(s), remaining
rep(s)	repeat(s), repeated, repeating
rnd(s)	round(s)
RH	right-hand
RS	right side (of work)
revsc	reverse single crochet (crab st)
sc	single crochet
sl	slip, slipped, slipping
ssk	[slip 1 st knitwise] twice from left needle to right needle, insert left needle tip into fronts of both slipped sts, knit both sts together from this position (decrease)
ssp	[slip 1 st knitwise] twice from left needle to right needle, return both sts to left needle and purl both together through back loops
st(s)	stitch(es)
St st	stockinette stitch
tbl	through back loop
tog	together
w&t	wrap next stitch, then turn work (often used in short rows)
WS	wrong side (of work)
wyib	with yarn in back
wyif	with yarn in front
yb	yarn back
yf	yarn forward
yo	yarn over
*	repeat instructions from *
( )	alternate measurements and/or instructions
[ ]	instructions to be worked as a group a specified number of times